Contents

Introduction

The boys whispered and made signs to Oliver. He stood up from the table and went to the master, with his bowl and spoon in his hands.
  'Please, sir,' he said, 'I want some more.'

Poor little Oliver's request for more food must be some of the most famous words that Charles Dickens ever wrote. We pity Oliver, a poor hungry boy, with nothing to eat except a bowl of thin soup every day. And we are angry with the unkind adults who control his young life but give him little food and no love.

Oliver's mother dies when he is born. His first years are cold and lonely – and then he runs away. But will he find a better life in London? Or will other adults use him for their own purposes?

Charles Dickens is one of the most famous writers in the English language. He was born in 1812. His father worked in a government office, but spent more money than he earned. When Charles Dickens was still a boy, his father was sent to prison because he could not pay his bills. In those days, people like him had to stay in prison until they found the money that they needed.

One result of this situation was that Dickens had experience of the unhappy life of many poor people, including children. During years of hard work in many unpleasant jobs, he met large numbers of people. Many of the descriptions in his books are descriptions of the men he worked for, the boys he worked with, and the London scenes of his own experiences.

As a young man, Dickens worked for a newspaper. He recorded, in note form, speeches and conversations in different parts of England, in courts of law, and finally in Parliament. During his time as a journalist, he had contact with members of the criminal population of London. Later he used what he learned in his books.

Dickens began to write short stories and descriptions for weekly and monthly magazines. Readers enjoyed these pieces, especially the amusing ones. *The Pickwick Papers* appeared in parts in 1836–37, and the public loved them. Mr Pickwick is a very simple, innocent character, writing in a funny way about the behaviour of the people of his time.

Because *The Pickwick Papers* were immediately popular, Dickens was soon able to stop his other jobs and make writing his only profession. His stories appeared in parts every week or every month, and people collected them to make books. They were usually complicated stories with a lot of characters, and readers waited anxiously for the next part. Later the stories were printed and sold as books. The most famous of these books are: *Oliver Twist* (1838), *Nicholas Nickleby* (1839), *The Old Curiosity Shop* (1841), *Dombey and Son* (1848), *David Copperfield* (1849), *Hard Times* (1850), *A Tale of Two Cities* (1859), and *Great Expectations* (1861).

Dickens's books were popular in the English-speaking countries on both sides of the Atlantic. In later years he travelled widely in Britain and America, reading from his books to an enthusiastic public. His sudden death in 1870 shocked thousands of people who were waiting for his next book.

Dickens wrote *Oliver Twist* in the years 1837–38. The dates are important because in 1834 Parliament passed a new law called the 'Poor Law'. The law said that there was work for everybody, so people without work or money were lazy. Local governments offered these people a workhouse, where they were given food and a bed. But the workhouse must not be comfortable or people might want to stay there instead of looking for work. So the workhouses were unfriendly places, and sometimes cruel men like Mr Bumble in *Oliver Twist* controlled them. Mr Bumble pretended to care for poor children like Oliver, but really he was only interested in the power of his job.

Another Act of Parliament was also beginning to have an effect on society. That 1829 Act formed a police force for London. When Dickens was writing *Oliver Twist*, the new police had become quite good at catching criminals. It was difficult for a murderer like Bill Sikes to escape, and all the criminals in *Oliver Twist* are afraid of the police. Punishments were also very hard. Even a young boy of Oliver's age could lose his life for a serious crime.

Governments at that time did not give much help to people who were old, ill, or had problems. But there were also kind people like Mr Brownlow, Mrs Maylie and Rose in *Oliver Twist* who were glad to help less fortunate people.

Charles Dickens was very successful when he was alive, and many of his books have become films and television programmes since his death. The amusing names of many of the people in his books have become very well-known. His characters often seem funnier, stranger, better or worse than men, women and children in real life. This adds humour to stories that are often very serious and sad. Through these characters we can learn a lot about the society of 19th century England. We can also enjoy a very good, exciting story.

Chapter 1   Oliver Asks for More

Among other buildings in a town in England, there was a house for poor people who had no money and nowhere to live. This was called the workhouse.

Oliver Twist was born in the workhouse. His mother, a young woman, lay ill in bed. A doctor and an old woman stood by her side. She lifted her head from the pillow.

'Let me see the child and die,' she said.

'Oh, you mustn't talk about dying yet,' said the doctor.

'No, dear,' said the old woman. 'You are too young to die.'

The young woman shook her head and held out her hand towards the child.

The doctor put the child in her arms. She pressed her cold white lips to its face, and then fell back.

'She is dead,' said the doctor.

'Yes, poor dear,' said the old woman, as she took the child away from its dead mother. 'Poor dear.'

'She was a good-looking girl,' said the doctor, as he put on his hat and gloves. 'Where did she come from?'

'She was brought here last night,' said the old woman. 'She was lying in the street. She had walked a long way and her shoes had holes in them. Nobody knows where she came from, or where she was going to.'

The doctor raised the dead woman's left hand.

'The usual story,' he said. 'I see that she has no ring on her finger. She wasn't married. Good night!'

He went home to his dinner. The old woman sat down on a chair in front of the fire and began to dress the baby. She dressed him in the very old clothes used for babies who were born in the

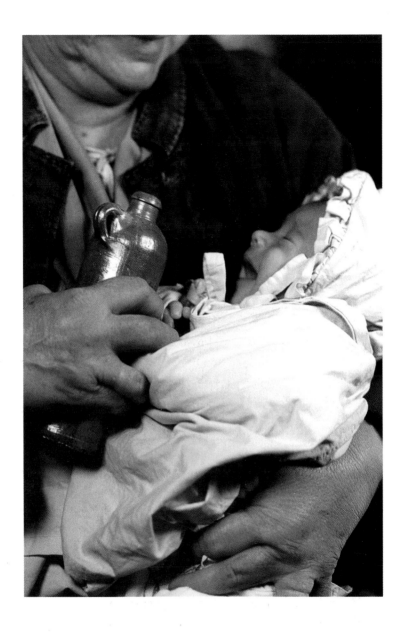

Oliver Twist was born in the workhouse.

workhouse. The child was an orphan, born into a world which had no love or pity for him.

No one was able to discover who the baby's father was, or what his mother's name was. Mr Bumble, an important officer in the town, invented a name for the baby. He chose the name Oliver Twist.

'We name the new babies here in order from A to Z,' he explained when people asked. 'I named the last one Swubble. This one is Twist. The next one will be Unwin.'

◆

At the age of nine, Oliver was a pale, thin child. He and the other workhouse boys never had enough warm clothes or food. They were given only three meals of thin soup every day. On Sundays they had a small piece of bread.

They were fed in a big hall. A large pot stood at one end of the room, and the soup was served by the master. Each boy had one small bowl of soup and no more. The bowls never needed washing, because the boys cleaned them with their spoons until they shone.

One day Oliver and his friends decided that one boy would walk up to the master after supper and ask for more soup. Oliver was chosen.

In the evening, the boys sat down at the tables. The master stood by the pot, and the soup was served. It disappeared quickly. The boys whispered and made signs to Oliver. He stood up from the table and went to the master, with his bowl and spoon in his hands.

'Please, sir,' he said, 'I want some more.'

The master was a fat, healthy man, but he went very pale. He looked with surprise at the small boy.

'What?' said the master at last in a quiet voice.

'Please, sir,' repeated Oliver, 'I want some more.'

The master hit Oliver with his spoon, then seized him and

'Please, sir,' he said, *'I want some more.'*

cried for help. Mr Bumble rushed into the room, and the master told him what Oliver had said.

'He asked for more?' Mr Bumble cried. 'I cannot believe it. One day they will hang the boy.'

He took Oliver away and shut him in a dark room. The next morning a notice appeared on the workhouse gate. Five pounds were offered to anybody who would take Oliver Twist.

Oliver was a prisoner in that cold, dark room for a whole week. Every morning he was taken outside to wash, and Mr Bumble beat him with a stick. Then he was taken into the large hall where the boys had their soup. Mr Bumble beat him in front of everybody. He cried all day. When night came he tried to sleep, but he was cold, lonely and frightened.

But one day, outside the high workhouse gate, Mr Bumble met Mr Sowerberry. Mr Sowerberry was a tall, thin man who wore black clothes and made coffins. Many of his coffins were for the poor people who died in the workhouse.

'I have prepared the coffins for the two women who died last night,' he said to Mr Bumble.

'Good,' said Mr Bumble. 'You will be rich one day, Mr Sowerberry! Do you know anybody who wants a boy? And five pounds?' He raised his stick and pointed to the notice on the gate.

Chapter 2   He Goes Out to Work

The arrangements were soon made, and Mr Bumble took Oliver to Mr Sowerberry's shop that evening. Oliver did not want to go.

'I will be good, sir!' he said. 'I am a very little boy and it is so – so – lonely! Please don't be angry with me, sir!' To Mr Bumble's surprise, Oliver had tears in his eyes. He told the boy not to complain, to dry his eyes and to be good. He took Oliver's hand, and they continued walking in silence.

To Mr Bumble's surprise, Oliver had tears in his eyes.

Mr Sowerberry had closed the shop, and he was writing by the light of a candle when they arrived.

'Here, Mr Sowerberry, I have brought the boy,' said Mr Bumble. Oliver bowed.

'Oh, that is the boy, is it?' said Mr Sowerberry. 'Mrs Sowerberry, come here, my dear.' A short thin woman with a narrow face came out from a little room behind the shop. 'My dear,' said Mr Sowerberry, 'this is the boy from the workhouse that I told you about.'

Oliver bowed again.

'Oh!' said the woman. 'He is very small.'

'Yes, he is rather small!' said Mr Bumble. 'But he will grow, Mrs Sowerberry, he will grow.'

'Yes, I expect he will,' said the lady angrily, 'on our food and our drink. Here, get downstairs, you little bag of bones. You can have some of the cold meat that we saved for the dog. The dog hasn't come home since this morning.'

Mrs Sowerberry opened a door and pushed Oliver down some stairs into a dark room.

Oliver's eyes shone at the thought of meat. They gave him a plate of the dog's food, and he ate very quickly. Mrs Sowerberry was not pleased that he was so enthusiastic.

'Come with me,' she said, taking a dirty lamp and leading him upstairs again. 'Your bed is in the shop. You don't mind sleeping among the coffins? But it doesn't matter whether you mind or not. You can't sleep anywhere else.'

Oliver was left alone in the shop full of coffins. He put the lamp down and looked around him. The shapes of the black boxes looked like the ghosts of dead people. The room smelt of death. He was alone in a strange place. He climbed quickly into his narrow bed and fell asleep.

The next morning he heard a loud knocking noise outside the shop door. 'Open the door!' cried a voice.

'I am coming, sir,' replied Oliver, turning the key.

A large boy was sitting in front of the house, eating bread and butter. He had small eyes and a red nose.

'Did you knock?' asked Oliver.

'I did.'

'Do you want a coffin?' asked Oliver innocently.

'You don't know who I am, Workhouse?' said the boy. 'I am Mr Noah Claypole, and you will work under me. Open the windows, you lazy boy!'

He kicked Oliver, and entered the shop. Noah was a poor boy, but not from the workhouse. He knew who his parents were. His mother washed clothes, and his father was a soldier who was always drunk. Other boys were rude to him, so he was glad that Oliver had come. Now he could be rude to Oliver.

Chapter 3   He Runs Away

Noah Claypole made life very unpleasant for Oliver. Mr Sowerberry tried to be his friend, so Mrs Sowerberry was his enemy. There was a lot of illness in the town, and Mr Sowerberry had a lot of business. He took Oliver with him when he collected the dead bodies, but Oliver did not like his new job very much.

One day Noah was trying to make Oliver cry. He pulled his hair hard and hit his ears.

'How is your mother, Workhouse?' he said.

'She is dead,' replied Oliver, and his face went pink. 'Don't say anything about her to me.'

'What did she die of?' asked Noah.

'Of a broken heart, some of our old nurses told me,' replied Oliver. 'Don't say anything more about her!'

'Don't be rude, Workhouse. We all pity you, Workhouse, but your mother was a bad woman. You know she was!'

'What did you say?' asked Oliver.

'A bad woman, Workhouse,' repeated Noah.

Red with anger now, Oliver seized the bigger boy by his neck, shook him and then threw him to the ground.

Oliver's unhappy life had made him a quiet, sad boy, but the insult to his mother had upset him. He stared angrily at Noah, who was still lying on the ground.

'He will murder me!' cried Noah. 'Help, Mrs Sowerberry! Oliver has gone mad!'

Mrs Sowerberry ran into the kitchen, caught Oliver and scratched his face. Noah got up and hit him from behind. When they were tired and could not tear and scratch and beat him any more, they carried Oliver to a dark room and shut him in there.

Mrs Sowerberry sat down and began to cry. 'He might murder us all in our beds,' she said. 'But what shall we do? Mr Sowerberry isn't at home. Run to Mr Bumble, Noah. Tell him to come here immediately.'

Noah found Mr Bumble at the workhouse.

'Oh, Mr Bumble, sir!' cried Noah, 'Oliver, sir, Oliver has—'

'What? What?' asked Mr Bumble, with a look of pleasure in his eyes. 'He hasn't run away, has he, Noah?'

'Not run away, sir, but he attacked me and tried to murder me, sir. And then he tried to murder Mrs Sowerberry, sir. Oh, the terrible pain!' And Noah showed signs of suffering badly from Oliver's attack.

'My poor boy,' said Mr Bumble. 'I will come now.'

He took his stick and walked with Noah to Mr Sowerberry's shop. He went to the door of the dark room and said in a deep voice, 'Oliver!'

'Let me out!' cried Oliver from the inside.

'Do you know this voice, Oliver?' asked Mr Bumble.

'Yes,' answered Oliver.

'Aren't you afraid of it?'

'No!' said Oliver in a brave voice.

Mr Bumble was very surprised by this answer. He stood back from the door and looked at the others.

'Oh, Mr Bumble, he must be mad,' said Mrs Sowerberry. 'No boy speaks to you like that.'

'He isn't mad,' said Mr Bumble after a few moments' deep thought. 'The trouble is – meat!'

'What?' said Mrs Sowerberry.

'Meat, Mrs Sowerberry, meat,' said Mr Bumble. 'If you fed him only on soup, as we do in the workhouse, he wouldn't behave like this!'

'Oh!' said Mrs Sowerberry. 'This is the result of my kindness.'

'Leave him in there for a day or two,' said Mr Bumble. 'Give him soup and nothing else in future, Mrs Sowerberry. He comes from a bad family.'

At this moment Mr Sowerberry arrived. He wanted to be kind to Oliver, but his wife's tears forced him to beat Oliver. He hit him hard and then shut him in the dark room again. At night Oliver was ordered upstairs to his bed in the shop.

When he was alone in the silence of the shop, Oliver began to cry for the first time. All day he had listened to their cruel words and suffered their beatings without any tears. But now he fell on his knees on the floor, hid his face in his hands, and started to weep.

For a long time he stayed like that, without moving. Then he opened the door and looked out. It was a cold, dark night. The stars seemed farther from the earth than he had ever seen them before. He shut the door, tied up his few clothes in a handkerchief, and sat down to wait for morning.

When the first light of day showed through the windows, he opened the door again. After one quick, frightened look around him, he closed the door behind him and was out in the open street.

Chapter 4   London

Oliver looked to the right and to the left. He did not know where to go. He remembered that vehicles and horses went up the hill as they left the town. He remembered walking along this path with Mr Bumble, and he took the same road. Soon he passed the workhouse. Outside, a small child was working in the garden.

Oliver stopped. It was Dick, one of his old friends. He was very glad to see him before he left. They had been hungry and beaten and locked up together many times. The boy ran to the gate and pushed his arms through the bars.

'You mustn't say that you saw me, Dick,' said Oliver. 'I am running away. They beat me and were cruel to me. I am going to try and find a better life, somewhere far away. I don't know where! You are very pale!'

'I heard the doctor tell them that I was dying,' replied the child with a faint smile. 'I am very glad to see you, but don't stop, don't stop!'

'Yes, yes, I will, to say goodbye to you,' replied Oliver. Dick climbed up the gate and put his arms around Oliver's neck and kissed him.

'Goodbye! God bless you!' he said. It was the first time in Oliver's sad little life that another person had blessed him, and he never forgot it.

It was eight o'clock now, and Oliver ran. He was afraid that they might follow him and catch him. At last he sat down by a big stone. The stone showed that it was just seventy miles from that place to London. London! That great city! Nobody could find him there. He had heard people talk about it. They said that a boy need not be poor and hungry there. It was a good place for a homeless boy to go, he told himself. He jumped to his feet and continued walking.

Oliver had a piece of dry bread, an old shirt and two pairs of socks. He had a penny, too, that Mr Sowerberry had given him one day when he had been pleased with Oliver's work.

'But these won't help me to walk seventy miles in the winter time,' he thought.

He walked twenty miles that day. He ate only the piece of dry bread, and drank water that people gave him along the road. When night came, he slept in a field. He was frightened at first, and very cold and hungry. But he was tired, and he soon fell asleep and forgot his troubles.

Next morning he had to spend his penny on bread. He walked twelve miles that day. Another night in the cold air made him feel worse. His feet hurt, and his legs were weak.

As the days passed, he grew weaker and weaker. A man gave him a meal of bread and cheese, and an old lady gave him food and some kind words. Without these, Oliver imagined, he would die on the road.

Early on the seventh morning, Oliver walked slowly into the little town of Barnet, a few miles from London. The streets were empty. Oliver sat on a doorstep. He was covered in dust, and there was blood on his feet.

Soon people began to pass, but no one offered to help him. He watched a coach and horses go past. It was strange, he thought, that it could travel the distance to London in a few hours. It had taken him a whole week to walk. He did not know what to do, so he just sat there.

Then he saw a boy looking at him. The boy had passed Oliver once and then returned. Oliver raised his head and looked at him. The boy walked across the road to Oliver.

'Hello! What is the trouble?'

He was a strange boy. He was about Oliver's age, but he behaved like a man. He wore a man's coat, which reached nearly to his feet, and a man's hat.

'What is the matter?' he asked Oliver.

'I am very hungry and tired,' said Oliver. 'I have been walking for seven days.' His eyes filled with tears.

'Seven days!' said the boy. 'Oh, you need food. I will pay for you. Get up now!'

He helped Oliver to stand up, and took him to an inn. There he bought some bread and meat and something to drink. Oliver had a good meal with his new friend.

'Are you going to London?' asked the strange boy, when Oliver had finished at last.

'Yes.'

'Have you got anywhere to stay? Any money?'

'No. Do you live in London?' asked Oliver.

'Yes, I do, when I am at home. I suppose you want somewhere to sleep tonight?'

'Yes,' answered Oliver. 'I haven't slept under a roof since I left the country.'

'Don't worry about it,' said the boy. 'I am going to London tonight, and I know an old gentleman who will give you a bed for nothing. He knows me very well.'

Oliver learned that the boy's name was Jack Dawkins. As Jack refused to enter London before dark, they did not reach the city until nearly eleven o'clock. Oliver followed him down a narrow street into one of the dirtiest places that he had ever seen. The people looked dirty, and some were drunk.

Oliver began to think that he ought to run away. But suddenly Dawkins caught his arm, pushed open the door of a house and pulled him inside.

Dawkins helped Oliver up the dark and broken stairs. He threw open a door and pulled Oliver in after him.

The walls of the room were very dirty. Some meat was cooking over the fire. There was an old man standing by the fire. He was dressed in strange clothes and most of his evil-looking face was hidden by his red hair. Half the time his attention was

Oliver learned that the boy's name was Jack Dawkins.

on his cooking. The rest of the time he was watching a line on which a lot of handkerchiefs were hanging. There were rough beds side by side on the floor. Four or five boys were sitting round the table, smoking long pipes.

'Fagin,' said Jack Dawkins to the old man, 'this is my friend Oliver Twist.'

The old man took Oliver's hand and said that he hoped to become his friend too. Then the young men with the pipes came round and shook both Oliver's hands very hard, especially the hand in which he held his handkerchief. One young man was anxious to hang up his hat for him. Another put his hands in Oliver's pockets to empty them for Oliver before he went to bed.

'We are very glad to see you, Oliver,' said Fagin. 'Ah, you are looking at those handkerchiefs. We put them there ready to wash. Ha! ha! ha!'

The boys all laughed at this, and they began to have their supper. Oliver ate with them. Then they gave him a bed on the floor and he fell asleep immediately.

Chapter 5   Fagin

Late next morning, Oliver woke from a long sleep. There was nobody in the room except the old man. He was boiling some coffee for breakfast.

Although Oliver was not asleep, he was not completely awake. He watched Fagin through half-closed eyes. The old man thought that Oliver was still asleep. He locked the door and then he pulled out a box from a secret hole in the floor. He placed the box carefully on the table. He then sat down and took an expensive gold watch from the box. He took out six more watches and looked at them with pleasure. There were also beautiful rings and other lovely jewels in the box.

Suddenly he looked up at Oliver's face. The boy's eyes were watching with silent interest. Fagin knew that Oliver had seen what he was doing. He shut the box quickly, took a bread knife from the table and went over to Oliver.

'Why are you awake? What have you seen? Speak, boy! Quick – quick! For your life!'

'I wasn't able to stay asleep, sir,' said Oliver. 'I am very sorry. I have only just woken up.'

'Did you see any of these pretty things?' said Fagin.

'Yes, sir.'

'Ah!' said Fagin, putting down the knife. 'They are mine, Oliver. I am an old man now, and I have nothing else.'

At that moment Jack Dawkins came in with another boy called Charley Bates. The four sat down and drank the coffee and ate the hot bread and meat that Jack had brought home.

'Well, my dears,' said Fagin, 'I hope you have been at work this morning. What have you got, Dawkins?'

'Two purses,' said Dawkins, and he gave them to Fagin.

'Not very heavy,' said the old man, 'but well made. He is good at his work, isn't he, Oliver?'

'Very good,' said Oliver.

'And what have you got?' said Fagin to Charley.

'Handkerchiefs,' replied Master Bates, producing four.

'Well,' said Fagin, looking at them carefully. 'They are good ones but they are marked, Charley. So we must take out the marks with a needle. Oliver will learn how to do it.'

'Yes, sir,' said Oliver.

Charley Bates started laughing. 'He is innocent, isn't he?'

After breakfast the old gentleman and the two boys played a very strange game. The old man placed a silver box in one pocket of his trousers, a purse in the other, and a watch and a handkerchief in his coat pocket.

He then walked round and round the room with a stick, like an old gentleman in the street. He stopped at the door, pretending to look at a shop window. Then he looked round, worried about thieves. He often touched his pockets to see if he had lost something. He did this in a very funny way, and Oliver laughed until the tears came to his eyes.

All this time the two boys followed close behind Fagin. They moved out of his sight very quickly when he turned round. At last Dawkins stepped on Fagin's foot, while Charley Bates pushed against him from behind. In that one moment they took from him the silver box, purse, watch and handkerchief. If the old gentleman felt a hand in his pockets, he cried out. Then the game began again.

They played this game many times, but it ended when two young ladies, Bet and Nancy, arrived to see the young gentlemen. They stayed and talked for a little time, and then the old man

'*Well, my dears, I hope you have been at work this morning.*'

gave them some money and they all went out together.

'Have they finished work, sir?' asked Oliver.

'Yes,' said Fagin, 'unless they find more work while they are out. Is my handkerchief hanging out of my pocket?'

'Yes, sir,' said Oliver.

'See if you can take it out, like the boys this morning. I mustn't feel anything.'

Oliver had watched the others carefully. He held up the bottom of the pocket with one hand, and pulled the handkerchief out of it with the other hand.

'Has it gone?' cried Fagin.

'Here it is, sir,' said Oliver, showing it in his hand.

'You are a good boy, my dear,' said Fagin. 'And now come here. I will show you how to take the marks out of the handkerchiefs.'

Chapter 6   Oliver Among the Thieves

Day after day Oliver stayed in Fagin's room, taking the marks out of handkerchiefs. Sometimes, too, he played the game with Fagin's pockets. At last he began to want fresh air. He asked Fagin to let him go out to work with Dawkins and Charley Bates.

One morning Fagin allowed him to go. The three boys left the house, walking very slowly. Oliver wondered if they were going to work at all.

They were just coming out of a narrow street into a square when suddenly Dawkins stopped. Putting his finger on his lips, he pulled his friends back.

'Quiet!' he said. 'Do you see that old man near the bookshop?'

'Perfect,' said Charley Bates.

Oliver looked at them in surprise. The two boys walked across the road and went close behind the old gentleman. Oliver followed them.

The old gentleman had white hair and gold glasses. He carried a stick under his arm. He had taken a book from a shelf in front of the shop and he stood reading it.

Oliver was shocked when he saw Dawkins put his hand into the old man's pocket and take out a handkerchief. Dawkins gave it to Charley Bates and they both ran away.

In a moment, Oliver understood the mystery of the handkerchiefs and the watches and the jewels and Fagin's games. He stood for a moment, full of fear, and then he too began to run.

The old gentleman put his hand in his pocket. He did not find his handkerchief, so he turned round. When he saw Oliver running away, he thought of course that the boy had stolen his handkerchief.

'Stop, thief!' he shouted, and ran after Oliver.

Everybody in the street joined him in the chase. 'Stop, thief,' they cried. Even Dawkins and Charley Bates began to shout 'Stop, thief!' and run after Oliver too.

Then someone hit Oliver and he fell to the ground. A crowd collected round him. Oliver lay, covered with dust, and bleeding from the mouth. He looked wildly at all the faces that surrounded him.

'Is this the boy?' they asked the old gentleman.

'Yes,' said the old gentleman, 'I am afraid it is. Poor boy! He has hurt himself.'

A police constable pushed through the crowd and seized Oliver by the neck. 'Get up!' he said.

'It wasn't me, sir. It was two other boys,' said Oliver. 'They are here somewhere.' But Jack and Charley had disappeared.

'Oh, no, they aren't,' said the constable.

'Don't hurt him,' said the old gentleman. 'I am not really sure that this boy took the handkerchief.'

The constable pulled Oliver along the street to the police station. Oliver was too frightened to speak.

'There is something in this boy's face that interests me,' said the old gentleman to himself. 'Is he innocent? Where have I seen a face like that before?'

Suddenly a man in an old black suit rushed into the police station. 'Stop, stop!' he cried. 'Stop a moment!'

'What is this? Who are you?' asked the constable.

'I own the bookshop,' replied the man, 'and I saw what happened. There were three boys – two others and this one. Mr Brownlow was reading and another boy took his handkerchief. This boy did nothing. He watched and looked surprised.'

'Then the boy must go free,' said the constable. He took his hands off Oliver, and the boy fainted.

'Poor boy, poor boy!' said Mr Brownlow, the old gentleman. 'Call a carriage, somebody, please. At once!'

A carriage came. Oliver was placed on one of the seats. The old gentleman got in and sat beside him. They rode away until the carriage stopped in front of a pleasant house in a quiet London street. Oliver was taken into the house and put to bed.

When Dawkins and Charley Bates arrived home, Fagin was waiting for them.

'Where's Oliver?' he said with an angry look.

The young thieves looked at him, but they said nothing.

'What has happened to that boy?' cried Fagin, quickly pulling Dawkins towards him. 'Speak or I will kill you!'

'A police officer took him away,' answered Dawkins.

He pulled himself free and took a knife from the table. Fagin picked up a cup and threw it at Dawkins's head. It missed him and nearly hit a man who was entering the room.

'Who threw that at me?' said a deep voice. He was a strong man of about thirty-five, with dirty clothes and angry eyes. A white dog followed him into the room. Its face was scratched and torn in twenty different places. 'What are you doing to those boys, Fagin?' the man said. 'I am surprised they don't murder you.'

'Who threw that at me?' said a deep voice.

'Quiet, Mr Sikes,' said Fagin. 'Don't speak so loud. You seem angry today.'

'Perhaps I am,' said Bill Sikes. 'Give me a drink, Fagin. And don't put poison in it,' he added as a joke.

While Sikes was drinking beer, Jack Dawkins told them about Oliver. He explained how he had been caught.

'I am afraid,' said Fagin, 'that the boy may tell the constable about us. We must find him.'

But none of them wanted to go near a police station.

The door opened and Bet and Nancy came in.

'Ah!' said Fagin. 'Bet will go, won't you, my dear?'

'Where?' said Bet.

'To the police station to find Oliver. He has been taken away and we must get him back.'

'No!' said Bet.

'Nancy, my dear,' said Fagin. 'What do you say?'

'No,' said Nancy.

'She will go, Fagin,' said Sikes, looking at her angrily.

So Nancy agreed to look for Oliver. In clean clothes and with a little basket, she looked very sweet.

'Oh, my poor, dear little brother, Oliver!' cried Nancy, pretending to weep. 'What has happened to him? Where have they taken him? Oh, please tell me!'

'Very good!' said Fagin. 'You are a fine girl, Nancy. Go and see the constable now.'

Nancy returned quickly. 'A gentleman has got him,' she said. 'Dawkins took the man's handkerchief. But the police don't know where he lives.'

'We must find him!' cried Fagin. 'Charley, you must watch that bookshop every day. I shall shut this house tonight. It isn't safe here. You know where to find me. Don't stay here, my dears. And find Oliver!'

Chapter 7   A Better Home

Oliver stayed in bed in Mr Brownlow's house for several weeks. He was quite ill. When he was a little better, he was able to sit in a chair and talk to Mrs Bedwin. She was an old lady who looked after the house for Mr Brownlow.

His new friends were very kind to him. Mrs Bedwin smiled at him and she fed him well.

One day he was carried downstairs to Mrs Bedwin's room. He stared at a picture of a lady on the wall.

'Are you fond of pictures, dear?' said Mrs Bedwin.

'I don't know,' said Oliver. 'I have seen very few. That lady has a beautiful face! But her eyes look so sad and they follow me when I move.'

'Oh!' cried the old lady. 'Don't talk in that way, child. You are weak after your illness. Let me move your chair, and then you won't see it.'

Then Mr Brownlow came down to see Oliver. As they were talking, Mr Brownlow looked at the picture.

'Mrs Bedwin!' he cried suddenly. 'Look there!' As he spoke, he pointed to the picture above Oliver's head and then to the boy's face. The eyes, the head, the mouth – they were exactly the same.

The next day, when Oliver came down to Mrs Bedwin's room for breakfast, the picture had gone.

'Why have they taken it away?' he asked.

'It seemed to upset you, child,' said Mrs Bedwin.

'Oh, no, it didn't upset me,' said Oliver. 'I liked it.'

'Well,' said the old lady, 'we will hang it up again when you are better.'

◆

Oliver soon grew strong and well. He was very happy in Mr Brownlow's house. Everything was quiet, tidy and clean. Mr Brownlow bought him new clothes and a pair of shoes.

One day Mr Brownlow called Oliver to his room. The room was full of books and Mr Brownlow was sitting at the window, reading. He told Oliver to come and sit down. He asked the boy what he wanted to do in the future.

'Please let me stay with you, sir,' cried Oliver. 'Please don't send me away! Let me be a servant in your house!'

'My dear child,' said the old gentleman. 'You can stay. I will never send you away unless you give me a reason.'

'I never, never will, sir,' replied Oliver.

'But let me hear your story, Oliver. Where did you come from? Who looked after you when you were small?'

Oliver began to cry, and then he started to tell Mr Brownlow about Mr Bumble and the workhouse. There was a knock on the door. It was Mr Grimwig, a friend of Mr Brownlow, and he had come to tea. Mr Grimwig was a large man in a blue coat and a white hat.

'Shall I go, sir?' said Oliver.

'No, stay here,' said Mr Brownlow. 'This is young Oliver Twist, the boy I told you about,' he said to Mr Grimwig. Oliver bowed.

Mr Grimwig looked at Oliver. He knew that his friend Mr Brownlow was very kind. He was afraid that the street boy might cheat or deceive him.

'So this is the boy, is it?' he said. 'And where does he come from? Who is he? When are we going to hear?'

'Tomorrow morning,' said Mr Brownlow. 'Come to me tomorrow at ten o'clock, Oliver, and we will talk about it.'

'Yes, sir.'

Mr Grimwig whispered to Mr Brownlow. 'You trust people too easily, my good friend.'

'He isn't lying to me,' said Mr Brownlow.

'If he isn't,' said Mr Grimwig, 'I will eat my head!'

At that moment, Mrs Bedwin came in with some books.

'These books must go back to the shop this evening, sir,' she said.

'Send Oliver with them,' said Mr Grimwig. 'If you can trust him, he will take the books back for you.'

'Yes, let me take them, please, sir,' said Oliver. 'I'll run all the way, sir.'

'Yes,' Mr Brownlow said to Oliver. 'You will have to pay the man at the bookshop four pounds. Here is a five pound note. You must bring me back a pound.'

'Yes, sir,' replied Oliver. He put the money safely in his pocket, placed the books carefully under his arm, bowed and left the room.

'He will be back in twenty minutes,' said Mr Brownlow. He took out his watch and put it on the table.

'Oh, you really expect him to come back, do you?' said Mr Grimwig. 'That boy has new clothes, good books under his arm and a five pound note in his pocket. He will join his old friends, the thieves, and laugh at you. If he returns to this house, I will eat my head!'

Chapter 8   Back Among the Thieves

Oliver was walking towards the bookshop when he heard a young woman shouting, 'Oh, my dear brother!'

He felt a pair of arms round his neck. 'Who is that?' he cried. 'Why are you stopping me?'

'I have found him!' cried the young woman. 'Oh, Oliver! Oliver! You are a bad boy. I have suffered so much!'

'Young Oliver?' cried Bill Sikes, coming out of a shop with

his white dog. 'Come home to your poor mother, you young fool. Come home at once.'

People watched and called to Oliver, 'Yes, you bad boy! Go home to your poor mother and father!'

'What are these books?' cried Bill Sikes. 'Have you been stealing?' He tore the books from Oliver and hit him.

What could one poor child do against all this? He was pulled by his collar through the narrow streets.

Night came. At Mr Brownlow's house, Mrs Bedwin stood at the open door. The two old gentlemen sat upstairs, waiting in silence with the watch on the table between them.

Nancy and Bill Sikes ran through the streets with Oliver. After half an hour they came to a very dirty, narrow street. Oliver did not know where he was. Sikes rang a bell, the door opened, and all three quickly went inside the house. It was dark inside. Sikes pulled Oliver down some stairs and opened the door of a dirty room at the back of a kitchen. Fagin and the boys were there.

'Look at his clothes, Fagin!' laughed Charley Bates. 'And books too! He is a little gentleman now!'

'I am glad to see you,' Fagin said. 'And you are looking so well. Jack will give you another suit, my dear – you mustn't spoil that Sunday suit.'

At that moment Jack Dawkins pulled out Mr Brownlow's five pound note from Oliver's pocket.

'What's that?' said Sikes, stepping forward as Fagin seized the note. 'That's mine, Fagin.'

'No, no, my dear,' said Fagin. 'Mine, Bill, mine. You can have the books.'

'If that money isn't mine I will take the boy back,' said Sikes. 'Nancy and I got him for you. Give us that money, you evil old man.' He took the note from Fagin's fingers. 'That is for our work,' he said. 'You can keep the books.'

'They belong to the kind old gentleman who took me to his

house,' said Oliver, falling on his knees at Fagin's feet. 'He looked after me when I was ill. Please send them back. He will think I stole them. Oh, please send them back!'

'The boy is right,' said Fagin. 'Ha, ha!' He laughed and rubbed his hands together. 'It couldn't be better for us!'

Now Oliver understood. He jumped quickly to his feet and shouted for help. He ran from the room, but Fagin and the other boys soon brought him back.

'Keep the dog away!' cried Nancy. 'He will tear the boy to pieces!'

Sikes pushed Nancy violently to the other side of the room.

'So you want to get away, my dear, do you?' said Fagin to Oliver, taking up a stick. 'You want to get help? You would like to send for the police perhaps? We will soon stop that.'

He hit Oliver hard. He was raising the stick for a second blow when Nancy rushed forward, pulled the stick from his hand and threw it into the fire.

'You've got the boy!' she cried. 'What more do you want?'

'Keep quiet!' shouted Bill Sikes.

'Women cause a lot of trouble,' said Fagin, 'but we need them for our work. Charley, take Oliver to bed.'

Bates led Oliver into the next room. He gave him a dirty old suit and took his new clothes away from him. Then he shut the door behind him and left Oliver alone in the dark.

◆

Fagin kept Oliver in the house for nearly a week. He reminded Oliver that without Fagin he would still be very hungry or even dead. He told him about a boy who had run away from him. Sadly he had been hanged – a very unpleasant death. Oliver was filled with fear as he listened to Fagin's words.

Then Fagin smiled at Oliver and said that if he worked hard for him, they would be very good friends. Oliver thought about Mr Brownlow, his good, kind friend.

'What will he think of me?' Oliver asked himself sadly.

One cold, wet night, Fagin left the house. He went down the dark street and knocked at the door of another house.

'Who is there?' said a man's voice.

'Only me, Bill, only me, my dear.'

'Come in,' said Sikes. They both had a glass of wine, then sat down to talk about business.

'I have come about the house at Chertsey,' said Fagin, rubbing his hands. 'When are we going to steal the silver from it?'

'We can't do it as we planned,' said the burglar. 'Toby Crackit has been staying near the place for more than two weeks now. None of the servants will agree to help him. Will you give me fifty pounds extra if the work is done from the outside?'

'Yes,' said Fagin.

'Then we can do it when you like,' said Sikes. 'Toby and I climbed into the garden the night before last. The house is shut at night like a prison. But there is one small window that we can open. We need a small boy to get through it.'

'Oliver is the boy for you, my dear,' said Fagin. 'He must start working for his bread, and the other boys are too big. He will do anything, Bill, if you frighten him enough.'

Chapter 9   Bill Sikes

When Oliver woke up in the morning he was surprised to find a new pair of shoes by his bed. His pleasure soon disappeared when he heard that he was going to see Bill Sikes.

'Why am I going?' he asked Fagin anxiously.

'Wait until Bill tells you,' said Fagin. 'Be careful, Oliver. Bill Sikes is an angry man. Do what he tells you.'

Oliver was terribly afraid. Falling on his knees, he prayed to God to save him.

Nancy came in. She turned very white when she saw Oliver

praying, and she covered her face with her hands.

'Nancy!' cried Oliver. 'What is it?'

'Nothing,' said Nancy. 'Now, dear, are you ready? You must come with me to Bill. You must be good and quiet. Give me your hand.'

'So you have got the boy,' said Sikes when Nancy arrived. 'Did he come quietly?'

'Like a baby,' said Nancy.

'I am glad to hear it,' said Sikes. 'Come here, boy, and let me talk to you.' He pulled off Oliver's hat and threw it in a corner. 'Now, do you know what this is?' he asked, taking up a pistol which lay on the table.

'Yes, sir,' said Oliver.

Sikes put bullets into the pistol.

'Now it is ready to use,' he said when he had finished.

'Yes, sir,' said Oliver.

'Well,' said Sikes, pressing the pistol against Oliver's head. 'If you speak a word when you are outside, I will shoot you in the head immediately. Do you hear?'

Sikes woke Oliver up at five o'clock the next morning. It was still dark outside, and rain was falling against the windows. After a quick breakfast, Sikes and the boy hurried through the streets.

The city was waking up. The inns and shops were opening for business, and people were going to work. The young boy had never seen so many people or so much activity.

Sikes pulled Oliver along by his hand. 'Hurry now!' he said, looking up at the clock of a church.

Daylight came as they reached the country roads. In the afternoon they came to an old inn, and Sikes ordered some dinner by the kitchen fire.

They continued their journey. The night was very cold and not a word was spoken. They walked across the fields until the poor tired boy saw the lights of a town.

'So you have got the boy,' said Sikes when Nancy arrived.

At a bridge Sikes turned suddenly. He left the path and went down to an old ruined house.

'Hello!' cried a loud voice when they were inside.

'Don't make such a noise,' said Sikes, closing the door. 'Show a light, Toby.'

A man appeared, holding a candle in his hand. He had red hair and big boots and some large rings on his dirty fingers.

'I am glad to see you, Bill,' said Toby Crackit. 'Is this the boy?'

'One of Fagin's,' said Sikes. 'Oliver Twist. Give us something to eat and drink while we are waiting.' He turned to Oliver. 'Sit down by the fire and rest, boy,' he said. 'You will have to go out with us again tonight.'

Oliver looked silently at Sikes and sat with his head in his hands. He was very tired and he did not really know what was happening.

Later, when the two thieves were ready, they went out with Oliver between them.

'Take his other hand, Toby. Let's go,' said Sikes.

They went quickly through the town, and then stopped in front of a house with a wall all round it. Toby Crackit quickly climbed to the top of the wall.

'The boy next,' he said. 'Lift him up. I will hold him.'

Sikes caught Oliver under his arms. In three or four seconds he and Toby were lying on the grass on the other side. Sikes followed them over the wall immediately.

Now, for the first time, Oliver understood that they were planning to enter the house – to steal and perhaps to murder. He fell to his knees in fear.

'Get up!' said Sikes angrily, taking the pistol from his pocket. 'Get up or I will shoot you through the head.'

'Oh, please let me run away and die in the fields,' cried Oliver. 'Don't make me steal!'

Sikes put the pistol to Oliver's head, but Toby took it from him and put his hand over the boy's mouth.

'Quiet!' he whispered. 'Don't shoot here. If the boy says another word, I will hit him on the head.'

He and Sikes took Oliver to the back of the house and they opened a small window.

'Now listen,' whispered Sikes to Oliver. He took a lamp from his pocket and lit it. 'I am going to put you through there. Take this light, go up the steps and along the little hall to the door. Open it and let us in.'

He stood on Toby's bent back and lifted Oliver through the window.

'Take this lamp,' he said. 'Can you see the stairs?'

'Yes,' whispered Oliver, shaking.

Sikes pointed to the door. 'If you don't open it, I will shoot you!' he warned. 'Now go.'

Oliver had decided that he would go upstairs from the hall and wake the family. He did not mind if he died. With this idea in his mind, he took one step forward.

'Come back!' cried Sikes. 'Back! Back!'

Frightened by this loud cry, Oliver dropped his lamp.

A light appeared at the top of the stairs, and he saw two men. There was another cry, a loud noise, a sudden light and smoke, and Oliver fell back. He had been shot.

Sikes reached out and seized Oliver before the smoke had cleared away. He fired his own pistol after the men, who were already running away. He pulled Oliver quickly through the window.

'Give me a coat, Toby,' he said. 'They have hit him.'

Then came the noise of a bell ringing. Men were shouting. Oliver was carried quickly across the ground. Then he fainted and he saw and heard nothing more.

Sikes rested the body of Oliver Twist across his knee. Then he shouted to Toby Crackit, 'Come back and help me carry the boy.'

But men were already climbing over the gate into the field. There were dogs with them too.

'They are chasing us!' cried Toby. 'Drop the boy!'

Toby disappeared. Sikes threw a coat over Oliver and ran.

The two servants from the house came to the middle of the field. They looked round.

'I can't see them,' one said. 'We should go home now.'

'Yes, Mr Giles,' said the other man. His face was white.

'You are afraid, Brittles,' said the first man, whose face was even whiter.

'We are both afraid. It is normal,' replied Brittles.

The air became colder as the sky grew light. The rain came down heavily. Still Oliver lay on the cold wet ground, where Sikes had left him.

Chapter 10   Oliver is Safe Again

Morning came and at last Oliver woke up. His left arm, covered in blood, hung at his side. He could not lift it. He was very weak, and he cried with the pain.

He knew that he had to move, so he got up slowly and walked to the nearest house.

'Perhaps the people in that house will feel pity for me,' he thought. 'And if they don't, it will be better to die near people than in the open fields.'

Oliver pushed open the garden gate and went slowly across the grass. The pain got worse. He climbed the steps, knocked at the door and then fainted again.

At this time Mr Giles, Brittles and the other servants were having some early morning tea in the kitchen. Mr Giles was telling the servants what had happened in the night.

Suddenly there was a noise outside. The cook screamed.

'That was a knock,' said Mr Giles. 'Open the door, somebody.'

Nobody moved.

'It seems a strange time to knock,' said Mr Giles. 'Open the door, Brittles. We will all stand near you.'

They walked forward slowly towards the door. Brittles opened it, and there was poor little Oliver Twist.

'A boy!' cried Mr Giles. He pulled Oliver into the hall.

'Here is one of the thieves, madam!' he shouted up the stairs. 'I shot him, madam.'

'Giles!' said the sweet voice of a young lady at the top of the stairs. 'Is the poor man hurt?'

'I think he is dying,' shouted Brittles. 'Would you like to come down and look at him, miss?'

'Please be quiet,' said the young lady. 'I will speak to my aunt, and ask her what to do.'

She soon returned and said, 'Carry the thief to Mr Giles's room. Brittles must go to the town for the doctor.'

Some time later, a carriage stopped outside the gate. A fat gentleman jumped out, ran into the house and came quickly into the room.

'This is terrible!' he cried, as he shook hands with the ladies. 'My dear Mrs Maylie – in the silence of the night – and you too, Miss Rose. Terrible!'

'We are all right, Dr Losberne,' said Rose, 'but there is a poor man upstairs that my aunt wishes you to see.'

'Yes, Brittles told me,' said Dr Losberne. 'You shot him, Giles? Where is he? Show me the way.'

The doctor stayed in Mr Giles's room for more than an hour. His bag was brought up from the carriage. A bedroom bell was rung very often, and the servants ran up and down the stairs all the time.

At last Dr Losberne returned to the two ladies. 'This is a very strange thing, Mrs Maylie,' he said.

'He isn't in danger, I hope?' said the old lady.

'No,' replied the doctor. 'Have you seen this thief?'

'No,' replied the old lady.

'I was going to tell you about him when the doctor came in, madam,' said Mr Giles. He felt rather ashamed to say that he had shot a small boy.

'Rose wanted to see the man,' said Mrs Maylie, 'but I didn't allow it.'

'There is nothing to be afraid of,' said the doctor. 'He is quiet and comfortable now. Will you both come and see him while I am here?' The doctor led the way upstairs. 'Now,' he said, as he opened the door, 'what do you think of him?'

There, instead of an evil man, lay a small child. He was weak with pain and was in a deep sleep. His arm rested across his chest, his head lay on his other arm and his hair was spread over the pillow.

They looked at him in silence. Then the younger lady bent over him. As she brushed back Oliver's hair, her tears fell on his face. Oliver moved and smiled in his sleep.

'What can this mean?' said the older lady. 'I cannot believe that this poor child was the pupil of thieves!'

'Who can say?' answered the doctor. 'We find evil, like death, among the old and the young.'

'But at such an early age!' cried Rose. 'Has he ever known a mother's love or the happiness of a comfortable home? Oh, aunt, dear aunt, don't let them take this sick child to prison!'

'My dear love,' said the old lady, 'of course not!'

Hour after hour passed, and in the evening Dr Losberne told the ladies that Oliver was able to talk to them.

Their talk was a long one. Oliver told them the story of his life. He was often forced to stop, because of the pain and his weak condition. It was sad to hear about such suffering from the mouth of a sick child. But the gentle hands and loving smiles of the ladies helped Oliver. He felt calm and happy and peaceful.

◆

Oliver was quite ill and weak. His broken arm was painful, and the rain and cold had given him a fever. He was sick in bed for many weeks, but slowly he grew better. With tears in his eyes, he thanked the two sweet ladies for helping him. When the warmer weather began and there were new leaves on the trees, they prepared to leave the town house for a house in the countryside.

It was a completely new life for Oliver. Here roses climbed the walls of the old country house and the air was filled with the smell of beautiful flowers. The days were quiet, and he was not afraid when he went to bed at night.

Every morning he went to see an old gentleman who taught him to read better and to write. He went for walks with Mrs Maylie and Rose. He listened when Rose played the piano in the evenings and sang in her sweet, gentle voice.

He helped in the garden and he worked at his lessons too. He fed Mrs Maylie's birds and sometimes he got up at six in the morning to pick flowers for the breakfast table.

Oliver was really happy. The ladies looked after him so well and he loved them with all his heart.

Chapter 11   The Mysterious Stranger

Spring passed quickly and summer came. The sun shone. Nature was growing, full of life and energy. Oliver grew bigger and healthier, but he was still the same gentle, sweet boy that he had been before.

One beautiful, warm night Oliver and the two ladies took a longer walk than usual. When they returned, Rose sat down at the piano. After playing for a little time, her hands suddenly began to shake. Her face was very white.

'Rose, my love!' cried Mrs Maylie. 'What is the matter?'

'Nothing, aunt, nothing,' said Rose. 'I am rather tired. I shall go to bed now and be better tomorrow. Please don't worry.'

When morning came, Rose was worse. It was clear that she was suffering from a serious illness. Mrs Maylie's sadness was terrible.

'We must send for Dr Losberne at once, Oliver,' she said. 'I have written a letter to him. Will you take it to the inn for me? From there someone will ride at once with it to Dr Losberne at Chertsey.'

Oliver ran off immediately across the fields. He found the inn and arranged for the letter to be taken to Dr Losberne. He was worried and nervous until he saw the man take the letter and ride away with it on his horse.

He was coming out of the inn when he almost fell against a tall man in a black coat.

'Curse you!' said the man in a voice of terrible anger. 'What are you doing here?'

'I am very sorry, sir,' said Oliver. 'I was in a great hurry to get home. I didn't see you.'

The man moved towards Oliver, but before he could hit the boy he fell to the ground.

Oliver stared at the madman for a moment and then ran into the inn for help. Some men came and carried the person inside. Then Oliver ran away as fast as he could. He was very frightened by the stranger's mysterious behaviour.

Dr Losberne arrived late that night and went straight to Rose while Mrs Maylie and Oliver waited outside the bedroom. Rose was very ill, the doctor said.

In the morning the little house was lonely and quiet. Oliver went to the old church and sat down outside on the grass. He wept and prayed for Rose. He looked around at the beautiful countryside and heard the songs of the summer birds. It was impossible that Rose could die when everything was so glad and happy.

When he went home, Mrs Maylie was sitting in the living-room. Rose had fallen into a deep sleep. When she woke up, she would either get better or say goodbye and die.

At last Dr Losberne came out of the bedroom.

'How is Rose?' cried the old lady.'Tell me at once!'

'You must be calm, my dear madam,' said the doctor.

'Tell me, in God's name! My dear child! She is dead!'

'Thank God, no!' cried the doctor, with great feeling. 'She won't die.'

The old lady fell on her knees and prayed. It was almost too much happiness to accept. Oliver could not weep, or speak, or rest. He went out and picked some beautiful flowers for Rose's room.

Every day Rose grew better, but she was weak for a long time and could not leave her room. The windows were open now because she loved to feel the warm summer air. But there were no more evening walks, and Oliver spent much of the time in his own little room working at his lessons.

◆

One evening, Oliver sat and read his books. He felt tired. It had been a hot day and he was not really awake but was only half asleep.

Suddenly he seemed to see Fagin, pointing at him and whispering to another man,'That is the boy.'

'I know,' the other man seemed to answer.

The anger and hate in the man's voice made Oliver jump up. What was that? There – there – at the window – close to him – very close so he could almost touch him – there stood Fagin. And beside him, white with anger or fear, stood the man who had met him outside the inn.

It was only a second – and then they had gone. But they had seen him and he had seen them.

He jumped from the window into the garden, and called for help in a loud voice. The servants came running. Oliver could only say,'Fagin! Fagin!'

'Was it a man?' cried Mr Giles, taking up a heavy stick.'Which way did he go?'

'Over there!' cried Oliver.

Mr Giles ran off, and Brittles followed him. Oliver ran behind with Dr Losberne, who was taking a short walk. But they could not find the two men.

'It must be a dream, Oliver,' said Dr Losberne.

'Oh no, really, sir,' replied Oliver. 'I saw Fagin – I am sure of that. I saw them both as clearly as I see you now.'

'Who was the other man?' asked Dr Losberne.

'The man that I told you about. He was at the inn,' said Oliver.

'This is very strange,' said Dr Losberne.

They continued to search for the two men, but without success. The next day Mr Giles was sent to all the inns in the area, but no one could tell him anything about the strangers.

Chapter 12   Mr Bumble and the Stranger

Mr Bumble was sitting by the fire in the workhouse where Oliver was born. He was drinking his tea and reading the paper, when a tall, dark man in a black coat came to see him. It was the man that Oliver had seen at the inn, and later outside his window with Fagin.

'Mr Bumble,' said the stranger, 'you are an officer of the workhouse, aren't you?'

'I am now master of the workhouse, young man,' said Mr Bumble slowly and in an important voice.

'I want you to tell me something,' said the stranger. 'I won't ask you to do it for nothing. Take this now.'

As he spoke, the man put two gold coins on the table. Mr Bumble took them and put them in his pocket.

'Try to remember something, Mr Bumble,' said the stranger. 'Twelve years ago last winter something happened in your workhouse. A boy was born here.'

'Many boys!' replied Mr Bumble, shaking his head.

'There was one little boy with a thin face. He was sent out to work for a coffin-maker. Then he ran away to London.'

'Ah, you mean Oliver Twist!' said Mr Bumble. 'Yes, I remember him!'

'I want to hear about the old woman who looked after his mother,' said the stranger. 'Where is she?'

'She died last winter,' said Mr Bumble. 'She had a friend with her when she died – another old woman from the workhouse. She was told something.'

'How can I find her?' asked the stranger.

'Only through me,' said Mr Bumble.

'When?'

'Tomorrow.'

'At nine in the evening,' said the stranger, taking a piece of paper and writing an address on it. 'Bring her to me at this place and in secret.'

Mr Bumble looked at the paper and saw that it had no name on it. 'What name should I ask for?' he said.

'Monks,' answered the man, and walked quickly away.

◆

It was a hot summer evening. Mr Bumble went down to the river. An old woman was with him.

'The place must be near here,' said Mr Bumble, looking at the piece of paper by the light of his lamp.

'Hello!' said a voice from an old empty house. 'Come in!'

They went in. The man in the black coat closed the door behind them.

'Now,' said the stranger to the old woman, 'what do you know about the mother of Oliver Twist? What did your friend tell you on her death bed?'

'How much money is her information worth to you?' said Mr Bumble.

41

'It may be worth nothing or it may be worth twenty pounds,' said Monks. 'Let me hear it first.'

'Give me twenty-five pounds in gold,' said Mr Bumble.

Monks thought for a moment. Then he took some money from his pocket. He counted out twenty-five gold coins and gave them to Mr Bumble.

'Now,' he said. 'Let's hear the story.'

'When old Sally died,' said the old woman, 'she and I were alone.'

'Was there no one else near?' asked Monks. 'No one who could hear you?'

'No,' replied the old woman. 'We were alone.'

'Good,' said Monks.

'She talked about a young girl,' continued the woman, 'who had brought a child – Oliver Twist – into the world some years before. Old Sally told me that the young mother had given her something before she died. She had asked her, almost with her last breath, to keep it for the child.'

'And did she keep it for the boy? What did she do with it?' cried Monks.

'She kept it for herself. She never gave it to the child.'

'And then?'

'She sold it to me.'

'Where is it now?' cried Monks.

'Here,' said the woman. She threw a small bag on to the table. Monks tore it open. Inside a small gold locket there were two pieces of hair and a plain gold wedding ring.

'The ring has the word "Agnes" inside it,' said the old woman. 'That was the name of the child's mother.'

'And this is all?' said Monks.

'All,' replied the woman.

'Good,' said Monks. 'Now come with me. I will show you what I am going to do with this jewellery.' He led them down to the river. 'There!' said Monks, throwing the bag into the river. 'That is the end of that! And you two will say nothing about all this?'

'Of course, Mr Monks,' said Mr Bumble, bowing. 'You can trust us.'

Chapter 13   Nancy Learns a Secret

Bill Sikes lay on his bed, covered by his coat. He had been ill with a fever for several weeks. The dog lay beside the bed and Nancy sat near the window. She looked white and thin. Illness had not improved Bill Sikes's temper. When Nancy helped him from the bed to a chair, he cursed her and hit her. She turned away and tried to laugh, but there was a tear in her eye.

The door opened and Fagin came into the room.

'Now listen to me, Bill,' said Fagin. 'We have got to get Oliver back. He is worth a lot of money to me, Bill.'

'How can we get him back?' said Bill.

'He is staying with Miss Maylie and her aunt. And I think we have a chance now, Bill. They have come to London from the country and they are staying at a hotel near Hyde Park. We will try again, and Nancy will help us.'

'Nancy can go with you now,' said Bill. 'I want some money from you.'

Fagin did not want to give Sikes any money, but they eventually agreed on an amount. Then he and Nancy left to get the money.

'Now,' said Fagin when they reached his room. 'I will give you the money, Nancy.'

They heard the sound of a man's voice on the stairs.

'I was expecting this man,' whispered Fagin. 'Don't talk about the money, Nancy! He won't stay long.'

Fagin took the candle to the door. Monks stood there in his black coat. He stepped back when he saw Nancy.

'This is one of my young people,' said Fagin. 'Don't move, Nancy.'

Monks came in.

'When did you return to town?' asked Fagin.

'Two hours ago,' answered Monks.

'Did you see him?' asked Fagin.

'I did,' replied the other man. 'Let me have a word with you.'

Fagin led the way to the sitting-room, where they would be alone. Nancy quickly took off her shoes, followed them and stood quietly near the door. She listened to their mysterious conversation with great interest.

When Fagin came back, Nancy was ready to go home.

'You have been a long time, Fagin,' she said unhappily. 'Bill will be in a bad temper when I get back.'

'I couldn't help it, my dear. Business.'

He gave Nancy the money that Sikes had asked for, and they said goodbye.

Chapter 14   A Visit to Rose Maylie

The next day Bill Sikes felt a little better and Nancy went out to buy food and drink with the money from Fagin.

Sikes drank a lot, then fell back into a deep sleep.

'Ah!' whispered Nancy as she stood up. 'I must go now or I may be too late.'

She quickly put on her hat and went out without a sound. She hurried through the busy London streets to the richer part of the town, where the streets were much quieter. As the clock struck eleven, she entered the hall of a quiet family hotel near Hyde Park. She felt nervous and waited for a few moments before she moved towards the stairs.

'Now, what do you want here?' asked one of the servants. He saw that she was poor, pale and thin.

'I want to see a lady who is staying here,' answered Nancy.

'A lady! What lady?' answered the man, looking at Nancy carefully.

'Miss Maylie.'

'Come!' said the man, pushing her towards the door. 'You must leave now.'

'No!' replied Nancy. 'Please take a message for me. Tell her that a young woman wants to speak to her alone, and it is very important.'

The servant went up the stairs. He thought that Miss Maylie would refuse to see her. But soon he returned and asked Nancy to follow him.

'I am the person that you wanted to see,' Rose Maylie said in a sweet voice.

The kind voice and the gentleness of Miss Maylie surprised Nancy. She started to cry. 'Oh, lady, lady!' she said. 'If there were more people like you in the world, there would be fewer like me!'

'Please sit down,' said Rose. 'If you are in trouble I will be glad to help you.'

'Is that door shut?' asked Nancy. 'I took little Oliver back to Fagin's on the night when he left that gentleman's house. I live among thieves but I have never known any better life. You have never known hunger and cold and slept in the streets with no friends, dear lady!' Nancy wept.

'I pity you!' said Rose. 'I am so sorry for you.'

'Heaven bless you for your kindness,' said Nancy. 'Nobody knows that I am here. They would murder me if they knew. But I want to tell you something that I have heard. Do you know a man called Monks?'

'No,' said Rose.

'He knows you, and he knows that you are here,' said Nancy. 'That is how I found this hotel.'

'I have never heard the name,' said Rose.

'Then perhaps he has another name,' said Nancy. 'Last night I heard him talking to old Fagin. They know that Oliver is here and they are planning to catch him again. Monks intends to pay Fagin if Oliver becomes a thief again.'

'But why?' asked Rose.

'I don't really know,' said Nancy. 'But if Oliver is a thief, his life will always be in danger. Monks hates Oliver so much! He said that he had the young boy's money now and wished to see him dead. Monks said, "That will be the end of my young brother, Oliver."'

'His brother!' cried Rose.

'Those were his words, lady,' said Nancy. 'And now it is late. I must get back before they find out that I have gone.'

'Don't go,' said Rose. 'Stay here. You will be safe with me. Why don't we tell the police?'

'I must go back,' said Nancy. 'How can I explain to a sweet, innocent lady like you? There is one man among the thieves that I love. I cannot leave him.'

'But you have come here to help Oliver. And it was dangerous for you. Let me help you now!' cried Rose.

'You are the first person who has ever spoken to me in such a kind way. But it is too late for me!'

'I can't let you leave like this,' said Rose. 'What shall I do?'

'You must tell this story to someone who will advise you,' said Nancy. 'We must save Oliver.'

'Where can I find you again if I need to?' asked Rose.

'Will you promise me that you will come alone, or with the only other person who knows about me?'

'I promise,' said Rose.

'Then, if I am alive,' said Nancy, 'I will walk on London Bridge every Sunday night from eleven until the clock strikes twelve. And now goodbye, dear lady.'

Chapter 15   Old Friends Meet

Oliver wanted to see Mr Brownlow again, while they were staying in London. He had told the two ladies about his kindness.

So Rose went with Oliver. She decided to tell Mr Brownlow Nancy's secret. When they arrived at his house, she asked to see Mr Brownlow on very important business.

She left Oliver in the carriage with Mr Giles, and followed the servant into an upstairs room. There she met a kind old gentleman. There was another old gentleman in the room who did not look so kind.

'Mr Brownlow, sir?' asked Rose, looking from one gentleman to the other.

'That is my name,' said the one with the kind face. 'This is my friend, Mr Grimwig. Grimwig, will you leave us for a few minutes?'

Rose remembered what Oliver had told her about Mr Grimwig.

She said, 'I think Mr Grimwig knows the business that I wish to speak about.' Mr Grimwig bowed.

'I shall surprise you very much,' said Rose, 'but you were once very kind to a very dear young friend of mine. I'm sure that you will be interested to hear about him again. His name is Oliver Twist.'

'Well, well!' said Mr Brownlow. He and Mr Grimwig looked very surprised.

'A bad boy!' said Mr Grimwig, 'I'll eat my head if he isn't a bad boy!'

'He is a good boy,' said Rose quickly. 'He has a fine nature and a warm heart.'

'Tell us what you know about this poor child,' said Mr Brownlow. 'We are very interested in him.'

Rose described everything that had happened to Oliver. She told them too that Oliver had been sad that he could not see his dear old friend, Mr Brownlow.

'This makes me very happy, very happy!' said the old gentleman. 'But, Miss Maylie, you haven't told us where he is now. Why haven't you brought him with you?'

'He is waiting in the carriage at the door,' said Rose.

'At the door!' cried Mr Brownlow. He hurried out of the room and down the stairs without another word.

When he had gone, Mr Grimwig got up from his chair and walked up and down the room. Then, stopping suddenly, he kissed Rose.

'Don't be afraid,' he said, as the young lady stood up in shock. 'I am old enough to be your grandfather. You are a sweet girl. I like you. Ah! Here they are!'

He returned quickly to his chair as Mr Brownlow came in with Oliver. Mrs Bedwin came too, and Oliver jumped into her arms.

While Oliver and the old lady were talking and laughing and crying and kissing, Mr Brownlow led Rose into another room. There he heard the story of Nancy's visit to Rose.

'This is a very strange mystery,' said Mr Brownlow, 'and we will never understand it until we find this man, Monks.'

'Only Nancy can help us,' said Rose, 'and we cannot see her until next Sunday.'

Chapter 16   Midnight on London Bridge

It was Sunday night. The church clock struck eleven. Sikes and Fagin were talking but they stopped to listen. Nancy looked up and listened too. While the two men talked, she put on her hat and coat.

'Nancy, where are you going at this time of night?'

'I am not well,' said Nancy. 'I want to breathe some fresh air.'

'Put your head out of the window,' replied Sikes.

'I want it outside.'

'But you won't have it.' Sikes shut the door, pulled the key out of the lock, seized the hat from Nancy's head and threw it up to the top of an old cupboard.

'Let me go, Bill!' cried Nancy, sitting on the floor. 'Tell him to let me go, Fagin!'

'I think the girl has gone mad!' cried Sikes.

He pulled her to her feet and threw her into a chair. Nancy fought and cried until the clock struck twelve. Then she became quiet.

Fagin picked up his hat and said good night. Nancy went down the stairs with him, holding a candle to light the way.

'Nancy dear,' said Fagin. 'If he behaves badly, I will help you. You know me. We are old friends.'

'I know you well,' replied Nancy. 'Good night.'

She moved away from him as he tried to shake her hand. The door closed between them.

Fagin walked home, thinking, 'Nancy is tired of Bill and his cruel behaviour. Perhaps I can make her work for me against him. Perhaps I can even make her poison him. Where does she go at night? I must have her followed.'

◆

It was Sunday night again. The church clock struck a quarter to twelve. Two people were on London Bridge. One was Nancy. The other was a man called Noah Claypole. Noah had recently started working for Fagin and, on his orders, was hiding in the shadows.

Soon two more figures appeared – a young lady and an old gentleman.

'Come down the steps here,' said Nancy. 'I am afraid to speak to you on the public road.'

They went down the steps towards the river.

'This is far enough,' said Mr Brownlow. 'Why have you brought us to this dark place? Why couldn't we meet in another place where it is light?'

'I was afraid,' replied Nancy.

'You weren't here last Sunday night,' said Mr Brownlow.

'I couldn't come. I was stopped by force.'

'By who?'

'Bill – the man that I told the young lady about before.'

'Does he know that you are here now?' asked the old gentleman anxiously.

'No,' replied Nancy, shaking her head.

'Good. Now listen,' said Mr Brownlow. 'Miss Maylie has explained to me everything that you told her two weeks ago. At first I didn't think we could trust you. But now I believe that we can. First we must find this man Monks and learn his secret. Then we must be sure that Fagin is put in prison. Oliver can never be safe while Fagin is free. You must tell the police about Fagin.'

'I can never do that!' replied Nancy. 'Fagin is an evil old man – but I will never do it!'

'Tell me why,' said Mr Brownlow.

'Although he has led a bad life, I have led a bad life too. I trust him, and he trusts me.'

'Then,' said Mr Brownlow, 'put Monks in our hands and we will do nothing to Fagin without your permission. Tell us everything that you know about Monks.'

Nancy told him about an inn where they might find Monks. Then she began to describe him. She spoke quietly and they had to listen carefully.

'He is tall and dark, with wild eyes that are deep in his head. I think that he is young – about twenty-eight. When he walks, he looks over his shoulder all the time. He wears black clothes. On his neck there is–'

'A wide red mark like a burn?' cried Mr Brownlow.

'Do you know him?' said Nancy with a cry of surprise.

'I think so,' said Mr Brownlow. 'Thank you for telling us this. Now, how can I help you?'

'You can do nothing to help me,' replied Nancy.

'Come with us. By tomorrow morning you will be far away from those bad people.'

'No, sir. I hate my life, but I cannot leave it,' replied Nancy sadly. 'Now I must go! I am afraid that somebody will see me!'

Rose Maylie held out a purse.

'I haven't done this for money,' Nancy said. 'I have done it for Oliver and for you.'

'Please take the money,' said Rose. 'It may help you.'

'God bless you,' said Nancy. 'Now I must go. Good night, good night.'

Rose and Mr Brownlow went slowly up the steps to the bridge. When they had gone, Nancy sat at the bottom of the steps and wept.

Noah Claypole was running towards Fagin's house as fast as his legs could carry him.

Chapter 17   Nancy is Murdered

It was nearly two hours before sunrise, and the streets were silent and empty. Fagin sat waiting in his room. His face was white and his eyes were red. He was covered with an old blanket and there was a candle burning on the table. Noah Claypole lay on the floor, fast asleep.

Fagin's thoughts were terrible ones: hate for Nancy, who had dared to talk to strangers; anger that his plans had failed; fear of ruin and prison and death.

He sat without moving until he heard a footstep.

'At last!' he whispered. 'At last!'

He opened the door and came back into the room with Bill Sikes. Sikes carried a bag, which he put on the table.

'There!' he said. 'Take that.'

Fagin took the bag and locked it in the cupboard. He sat down again without speaking. He stared at the burglar.

'What is the matter?' shouted Sikes. 'Why are you looking at me like that?'

Fagin turned to the sleeping young man and woke him. 'Poor Noah,' he said. 'He is tired. He has been watching her for so long, Bill.'

'What do you mean?' asked Sikes.

Noah Claypole sat up and rubbed his eyes.

'Tell me what you told me before, Noah,' said Fagin. 'About Nancy. You followed her?'

'Yes.'

'To London Bridge?'

'Yes.'

'And there she met two people. A gentleman and a lady. She had been to see them before. They asked her to tell them about Monks. They knew where we meet. She told them everything, didn't she?' cried Fagin.

'That's right,' said Noah.

'And tell him what she said about last Sunday!'

'She told them that she couldn't come last Sunday because she had been stopped by force!'

Sikes became wild with anger. He cursed everyone. Then he pulled open the door and ran out.

'Be careful, Bill!' said Fagin. 'Don't be too violent, will you?'

When Sikes reached his room, he shut the door and put a heavy table against it.

Nancy was lying on the bed. She had been asleep. 'Oh Bill!' she said, pleased that he had returned.

'Get up!' said Sikes.

He picked up the candle and threw it into the fire. Nancy went to the window to open the curtain.

'Leave it!' shouted Sikes.

'Bill!' said the girl in a frightened voice. 'Why are you looking at me like that?'

The burglar watched her for a few seconds. Then he seized Nancy by her head and throat and threw her into the middle of the room.

'Bill! Bill!' she said. 'Tell me what I have done!'

'You know what you have done, you evil girl! You were watched tonight. You were followed to London Bridge.'

'Then don't take my life. I haven't forgotten my love for you! That gentleman and the dear lady will help us – I know they will. They have given me money. Let's leave this terrible place and lead better lives far away from here. It is never too late to be sorry for the past!'

She tried to put her arms around him, but Sikes seized his pistol. He realized that somebody might hear a gunshot so, with all his strength, he struck Nancy's face with the pistol.

Nancy fell. She was nearly blind with the blood that poured from her head. She raised herself to her knees, breathed hard and prayed to God for forgiveness.

It was a terrible sight. Sikes covered his eyes. Then he seized a heavy stick and hit her again.

Chapter 18   Sikes Escapes

As the sun came up over the city, Sikes tried to clean the blood from his clothes. The floor was covered with blood. Even the dog's feet had blood on them.

Then he went out, carrying the dog. He walked quickly through the city until he came to the country roads outside London. He lay down in a field and slept.

Morning and afternoon soon passed. In the evening, Sikes walked again. Where could he go for food and drink? At nine o'clock, he came to a village and went to the inn. He sat alone, throwing a few pieces of food to his dog as he ate.

When he came out, he saw a coach bringing letters from London. It passed him on the road and stopped at the little village post office. As he got nearer, Sikes could hear the guard talking to the man at the post office.

'People in London are talking about a murder,' said the guard. 'A terrible murder!'

'Man or woman?'

'A woman,' said the guard.

The coach drove away. As he walked, Sikes began to feel a terrible fear. Everything on the road – every tree, every shadow – seemed like a ghost. He imagined that there was blood everywhere. He could not stop thinking about his terrible crime.

'I can't spend another night alone in the fields,' he thought. 'I will go back to London. The police will never expect to find me there. Why can't I hide there for a week and then get away to France? Fagin will help me.'

Sikes began his journey back immediately. He went by different roads and he decided to enter the city by night.

'But the dog?' he thought. 'The police must guess that the dog is with me.'

He came near a small river. Picking up a heavy stone, he tied it to his handkerchief. The dog looked up into his master's face.

Sikes went down to the edge of the river. The dog did not follow.

'Come here!' cried Sikes. The dog came towards him, and then moved back. 'Come here!' cried Sikes again.

The dog stopped for a moment, then turned and ran away as fast as it could.

Sikes called and called, and then sat down and waited. But no dog appeared and at last Sikes continued his journey alone.

Chapter 19   Monks is Caught

Night was falling when Mr Brownlow stepped down from his carriage and knocked at his own door. Two of his servants came. They helped a second man from the carriage and took him into the house. This man was Monks.

'Now,' said Mr Brownlow, as they sat down, 'we must talk.'

'You were my father's oldest friend,' said Monks. 'How dare you kidnap me in the street and bring me here?'

'Yes, I was your father's oldest friend,' said Mr Brownlow. 'I also loved his beautiful sister, your aunt. I hoped to marry her, but she died young. For love of them, I wish to talk to you – Edward Leeford.'

'What do you want with me?' said the man who called himself Monks.

'You have a brother,' began Mr Brownlow.

'I have no brother,' said Monks.

'Listen to me,' said Mr Brownlow. 'I know your family history. I know about your father's unhappy marriage. I know how your father and mother separated. Your father was still young at the time, and later he met some new friends – a man and his beautiful daughter aged nineteen.'

'Why do I care about this?' asked Monks angrily.

'Your father fell in love with the daughter,' continued Mr Brownlow. 'Your father was very rich at that time. A member of the family had died and left him a lot of money. When your father died suddenly, all his money went to your mother, and to you, the son from his marriage to her. Your father came to see me just before he died.'

'I didn't know that,' said Monks.

'He came,' said Mr Brownlow, 'and he left with me, among some other things, a picture of this young girl. He loved her. And she loved and admired him, although she was young and weak. He asked me to look after the picture for him. He was going to take the young lady with him to another country. And then – he died.'

Mr Brownlow stopped for a moment.

'I looked for the girl after his death,' he said, 'but she had disappeared. I never saw her again. Her name was Agnes. Later her child was born in the workhouse. That child had the same father as you. He is your half-brother – Oliver Twist. I didn't know this until chance brought Oliver into my house.'

'What?' cried Monks.

'Yes,' said Mr Brownlow. 'Oliver stayed with me for a time. I didn't know who he was then. He was a dirty, poor, unhappy boy, but I saw that he was like the girl in the picture. You already know that he was taken away from me by terrible thieves.'

'I know nothing about that!' cried Monks.

'Really?' said Mr Brownlow. 'Let me continue. I lost the boy and couldn't find him. His mother was dead, so only you could help me. I tried for a long time to find you.'

'And now you have found me,' said Monks, getting up. 'You cannot prove that the boy is my brother.'

'In these past few weeks I have learned a lot,' said Mr Brownlow. 'You have a brother and you know it. Your father left a will which your mother destroyed. This will spoke of the future birth of a child, and money that should go to this child.'

'No!' shouted Monks.

'I know it all,' said Mr Brownlow. 'You have tried everything – every evil plan – to destroy Oliver. You told Fagin, your evil friend, that everything is lying at the bottom of the river. The jewellery that would help Oliver. A ring that your father gave to Oliver's mother. Her name was written inside with a space for his name – he hoped to marry her. Isn't this true?'

Monks was silent.

'I know every word that you and Fagin spoke,' cried the old gentleman. 'And there has been a murder because of it!'

'No, no,' replied Monks. 'I know nothing about that!'

'You also gave Fagin money.'

Eventually Monks said, 'When my mother died, she believed that a child had been born as a result of that relationship. I promised her that I would find the horrible little orphan! I found him at last. I wanted to destroy him, but that girl talked!'

'I won't tell the police,' said Mr Brownlow, 'but you must tell the whole truth. And Oliver must get his share of the money. You will sign some papers. And after that, you can go where you want. Do you agree?'

Monks walked up and down the room. He could not speak.

The door opened, and Mr Grimwig came in.

'News of the murder,' he said. 'They will catch the man tonight, they think. The police have seen his dog. There is a hundred pounds reward for him.'

'I will give fifty more,' said Mr Brownlow. 'What is the news of Fagin? Where is he?'

'He hasn't been caught yet,' said Mr Grimwig. 'But he will be.' Monks looked at the two men in terror. 'Mr Bumble has arrived,' continued Mr Grimwig. 'He is downstairs. Will you see him now?'

'Yes, in one moment,' said Mr Brownlow. He turned to Monks. 'Have you decided?' he said in a low voice. 'Do you agree to what I said?'

'Yes, yes, I agree,' said Monks. 'You will keep everything secret?'

'I will,' said Mr Brownlow.

Mr Grimwig led Mr Bumble into the room.

'I am very glad to see you, sir,' said Mr Bumble to Mr Brownlow. 'And how is our dear little Oliver? I always loved that boy like a son. Dear Oliver!'

'Now,' said Mr Brownlow, pointing to Monks, 'do you know this person, Mr Bumble?'

'No,' said Mr Bumble.

'Are you sure?'

'I have never seen him before.'

'And you didn't sell him anything? You never saw, perhaps, a certain piece of gold jewellery – a locket – and a ring?'

'All right,' Mr Bumble said. 'I did receive some money from this man. But you will never find the locket and the ring.'

'You will lose your position as master of the workhouse,' said Mr Brownlow. 'Nobody can trust you.'

Chapter 20   The Death of Sikes

Jacob's Island was in the Thames, where the river ran through one of the lowest, dirtiest and poorest parts of London. The old houses there were empty. They had no roofs, and the walls were falling down.

Toby Crackit and Charley Bates were hiding in one of these old houses. They were talking in frightened voices.

'When was Fagin caught?' asked Toby.

'At dinner time today. I hid and escaped up the chimney,' said Charley.

'They will hang Fagin, and Sikes too when they get him,' said Toby in a frightened voice. 'We are in real danger.'

'No one will find us here,' said Charley.

As they sat talking, they heard a noise on the stairs. Sikes's dog ran into the room. It was covered with mud and was very tired.

'What does this mean?' said Toby. 'Sikes isn't coming here, is he? I . . . I hope not.'

'No. He has probably left the country and the dog. Look – he must be without his master or he would be afraid.'

They gave the dog some water, then it lay down under a chair and went to sleep. The boys lit a candle and placed it on the table. They sat together, frightened, and waited.

Suddenly there was a knock at the door below. Toby ran to the window and looked out. His face went white.

'We must let him in,' said Charley, picking up a candle.

Sikes came in. His face looked old and tired, and he had not shaved for three days. He sat down and looked at the boys in silence. Eventually he spoke.

'When did that dog come here?' Sikes asked.

'Three hours ago.'

'The paper says that Fagin has been caught. Is it true?'

'True,' said Charley.

They were silent again.

'Curse you both!' said Sikes. 'Have you nothing to say to me?'

'You are evil!' shouted Charley Bates. 'I am not afraid of you! Toby may let you stay here, but I am not going to help you.'

Sikes threw him to the floor. His knee was on Charley's neck when there was another loud knock. There were lights outside, and voices.

'Open this door!'

'They are here! They have found us!' whispered Toby, pale with terror.

The voices outside grew louder. People were trying to climb the wall. Some called for ladders; others said they would burn the house down.

'The water!' cried Sikes. 'The water is low so I can get away on the river. Give me a rope, Toby, a long rope. The people are all at the front. I will drop down at the back.'

Toby pointed in fear at a cupboard where there was some rope. Sikes took the longest piece that he could find. He quickly went to the top of the house, climbed to the edge of the roof and looked over.

The level of the water was very low, and the river was just a stretch of mud.

The crowd outside shouted as Sikes appeared on the roof. The people at the front of the house ran round to the back to watch. At the same time, Sikes heard noises inside the house. The police were entering the building.

He tied one end of the rope tightly round the chimney. He tied the other end round himself.

'I can climb down nearly to the ground,' he thought, 'and then I can cut the rope and fall. My knife is ready in my hand.'

At that moment he looked behind him on the roof and shouted in terror.

'Those eyes again!' he cried. 'I can still see her eyes!'

He fell back and dropped off the roof. The rope suddenly moved and caught around his neck. He fell for thirty feet, and then there was a sudden stop. His body hung against the wall – the knife still in his hand – dead.

Chapter 21 The End of the Story

Fagin sat in prison. Looking at the floor, he tried to think. He began to remember the judge's words.

He fell back and dropped off the roof.

'Guilty,' the judge had said. Everybody in the court had shouted cheerfully. 'You will be hanged by the neck until you are dead.'

As it grew dark, Fagin began to think of all his colleagues who had died in this way. Some of them had died because of him. Many men had sat in that small room, waiting to die. This was his last night alive. Silence was broken only by the sound of the church clocks. Every bell brought him the same message. Death.

Suddenly the prison officer opened the door of the room.

'Somebody wants to see you, Fagin!' said the man.

Mr Brownlow came in with Oliver. Fagin moved to the farthest corner of the room, away from the visitors. He looked ill and frightened.

'You have some papers,' said Mr Brownlow, moving towards the old man. 'They were given to you by a man called Monks.'

'That is a lie,' replied Fagin.

'Please,' said Mr Brownlow in a very serious voice, 'don't say that now, when you are soon going to die. Tell me where the papers are. You know that Sikes is dead, and Monks has told us the truth. There is no more hope for you. Where are the papers?'

'Oliver,' cried Fagin, pointing his finger at him. 'Here, here! Let me whisper to you.'

'I am not afraid,' said Oliver.

'The papers are in a bag, in a hole a little way up the chimney in the sitting-room.'

The night passed. Outside the men were building the platform for Fagin's last moments. A crowd of people waited to watch Fagin die.

◆

Our story is nearly over. After Fagin's death, Charley Bates decided that an honest life was best. He began a new and happy life, working for a farmer.

Mr Brownlow took the papers that Fagin had kept for Monks. They proved that Oliver's father had left his son half of his property in his will. So the money was shared between Oliver and Monks. Mr Brownlow wanted to give Monks the chance to live a better life. Monks went to America but he wasted his money there and died in prison.

Mr Bumble lost his job as master of the workhouse. He became very poor, so he had to move into that same workhouse.

Noah Claypole continued his new profession, giving information about crimes and criminals to the police, and was very successful.

Oliver lived with Mr Brownlow as his son. The old man loved and protected his young friend, and they moved to a house in the country with old Mrs Bedwin. Their house was about a mile away from the home of Mrs Maylie and Rose.

Mr Giles and Brittles were still Mrs Maylie's servants. Dr Losberne went back to Chertsey, but after a few months he moved to the village too. In the church there was now a white stone with one word written on it: AGNES. It helped Oliver to remember his mother. Mr Grimwig often came down from London to visit them all, and they enjoyed themselves together very much.

ACTIVITIES

Chapters 1–4

Before you read

1 Answer these questions. Find the words in *italics* in your dictionary.
  They are all in the story.
  a What is an *orphan*?
  b Why did people live in a *workhouse*? Do you think it was a
    pleasant place? What position do you think the *master* had?
  c What happens to someone who is *hanged*?
  d What can you do at an *inn*?
  e When you *bow*, which part of your body moves?
  f What are these things for?
    a *candle* a *coach* a *coffin*
  g What happens when you:
    (i) *raise* something?
    (ii) *scratch* someone?
    (iii) *seize* something?
    (iv) *tear* something?
    (v) *weep*?
  h Is an *evil* person good or bad?
  i When someone *blesses* you, are they being kind or unkind?

2 Look at the picture of Mr Bumble on page 6. Describe him. What
  kind of person do you think he is?

After you read

3 Answer the questions.
  a What happens to Oliver after he asks for more food?
  b Is Oliver happy working for Mr Sowerberry? Why (not)?
  c What does Oliver do to Noah? Why?
  d How long does it take Oliver to get to London?
  e Who is Oliver's new friend?

4 Imagine you are Oliver. Describe how you feel on your journey
  to London.

Chapters 5–8

Before you read

5 What do you think will happen to Oliver while he lives with Fagin?

6 Find these words in your dictionary. Use them in the sentences below.

carriage constable deceive faint rub trust

   a He felt weak and ill, and then he ....

   b You can't .... strangers.

   c They travelled in a .... to the next town.

   d She .... her aching head.

   e We were .... by someone who pretended to be a friend.

   f The thief was taken away by the ....

After you read

7 Why does Fagin play a 'game' with the boys?

8 Work in groups of four. Imagine that you are Dawkins, Bates, Oliver and Mr Brownlow. Act out the scene in front of the bookshop.

9 Compare the ways in which Fagin and Mr Brownlow behave to Oliver.

Chapters 9–12

Before you read

10 Do you think Oliver will help Bill Sikes?

11 Oliver is going to meet a mysterious stranger. Who do you think it is? Is it a good person or a bad person?

12 Translate these sentences into your language. What do the words in *italics* mean? Look in your dictionary.

   a The old man *cursed* all his enemies.

   b She always wears the *locket* around her neck.

   c He *fired* his *pistol* and the other man fell to the ground.

   d Let's *pray* for all the poor orphans.

   e How much is your house *worth* now?

13 Is the burglary successful? Explain what happens.

14 Discuss the best adjectives to describe Rose Maylie.

15 Who is the mysterious stranger? Why does he visit Mr Bumble?

Chapters 13–16

Before you read

16 Chapter 13 is called 'Nancy Learns a Secret'. What do you think she will discover? What will she do next?

After you read

17 Why do you think:

    a Nancy stays with Bill Sikes?

    b Nancy visits Rose Maylie?

    c Rose listens to Nancy?

    d Monks is doing business with Fagin?

18 Work with another student.

    Student A: You are Fagin. Ask Charley Bates who Nancy met on London Bridge and what they talked about.

    Student B: You are Charley Bates. Tell Fagin what you saw and heard near London Bridge.

Chapters 17–21

Before you read

19 How might these things be important to the story? Check the words in your dictionary.

    a *rope*   a *will*

20 What do you think is going to happen to these characters?

    a Nancy

    b Bill Sikes

    c Fagin

    d Oliver

After you read

21 What happens at the old house near the river?

22 What happens to these characters at the end of the book?

    a Monks

    b Charley Bates

    c Mr Bumble

    d Oliver

Writing

23 Which character in *Oliver Twist* do you like best? Why?

24 Imagine that you live in Charles Dickens's time. Write a letter to a newspaper describing the life of a child in the workhouse and giving your opinion of it.

25 How do the women in the story behave towards Oliver Twist?

26 You are Charley Bates. Write about your old life among the thieves in London. How have you changed?

27 What reasons do readers have to hate these characters? Which do you think are evil? Which are weak?

    a Mr Bumble

    b Fagin

    c Bill Sikes

    d Monks

28 Write the conversation between Oliver's mother and old Sally when the dying woman gave the old woman the ring and the locket.

Answers for the Activities in this book are published in our free resource packs for teachers, the Penguin Readers Factsheets, or available on a separate sheet. Please write to your local Pearson Education office or to: Marketing Department, Penguin Longman Publishing, 5 Bentinck Street, London W1M 5RN.